LET IT

BURN

LET IT

Illuminate Your Life with Candles and Fragrance

SIR CANDLE MAN

CHRONICLE BOOKS

SAN FRANCISCO

BURN

OVE POTION

Mandarin
Lavender
Jasmine Blossoms

Library of Congress Cataloging-in-Publication Data available.

ISBN 978-1-7972-2208-0

Manufactured in China.

Design by RACHEL HARRELL.
Typesetting by FRANK BRAYTON.

10 9 8 7 6 5 4 3 2 1

Chronicle books and gifts are available at special quantity discounts to corporations, professional associations, literacy programs, and other organizations. For details and discount information, please contact our premiums department at corporatesales@chroniclebooks.com or at 1-800-759-0190.

CHRONICLE BOOKS LLC
680 Second Street
San Francisco, California 94107
www.chroniclebooks.com

For Saron & Julia, thank you
for striking the match that
started this candle journey,
and my beloved followers,
for keeping the flame alive.

welcome to the candle lifestyle

Greetings!

This looks like a book about candles. And while that's true, it's also so much more than that.

We all find joy in indulging our senses. We eat delicious foods to satisfy our taste buds. We feast our eyes on thoughtful art or jaw-dropping landscapes. We listen to the music we love. For touch, well . . . we touch, I guess. (Haha.) But nothing is as evocative as smelling beautiful fragrances in perfumes and in nature.

In our particularly frenzied world, we are in a lot of spaces on any given day, and all these places have different energies. Some energies are positive and uplifting, while others are negative and bring you down. Candles and their scents can create the exact energy you wish to sur-round yourself with.

The early days of the COVID-19 pandemic were a dark time for many of us. In the midst of the isolation, I found myself needing light, fun, and love. While others chose to bring joy into their lives with food, DIY projects, new home decor, and game nights, collecting and living with candles became the light I needed to bring joy and creativity back into my life.

Although I had started buying candles intentionally the year before, my love of candles became a full-blown love affair after the pandemic began. The best luxury candles have stories, creativity, and passion infused in them. I would spend my nights reading about perfumers, understanding the artwork, diving deep into fragrance notes, and sharing what I learned online as Sir Candle Man.

Not only have candles made my life smell amazing, but they have also helped me learn the importance of self-care rituals, the importance of having a creative escape, the importance of always learning, the importance of sharing what you love with others, and, mostly, the importance of self-love. I dedicated myself to learning a whole new craft, found a new passion, made new fragrance friends, and found gifts I could give to people; all of this was also a way for me to pour love back into myself. The darkness faded away and my life was literally and figuratively lit up in the best possible way.

In this book, you will learn everything you need to know about using candles to bring light into your own life. You'll learn what to look for when you're shopping for candles, how to think about the best fragrances for your home, and how to create the vibes you want using candles. You'll learn how to accessorize and style your candles and how to incorporate candles into your wellness routines. But above all, I hope you'll learn that you have the power to make your life beautiful by leaning into your passions. This book is about candles, but the lessons apply to all parts of your life. Find something you love, commit to it deeply, and a world of blessings will open up and enrich your life beyond measure.

Scented candles have made my sacred spaces smell beautiful, but they have also made my life beautiful. Candles have given me the power to create any space I want and feed the deep need I have for adding more self-care moments to my routine. I hope that candles can do the same for you, and that this book will show you how.

Every time you light a candle, you are choosing to bring light into your life.

Love,
Sir Candle Man

becoming sir candle man

How did I go from being a tech executive by day to a candle influencer by night? Well, one day in 2018, a candle changed my life. I went to Paris that year to celebrate my birthday with my friends and to attend a Beyoncé concert. One afternoon, we decided to go shopping. As I was waiting for my friends in Galeries Lafayette, a big department-store chain in France, I stumbled upon a perfume stand. I had time to kill as my friends were trying on clothes, so I began exploring the fragrance section. After trying a few perfumes, I smelled a candle and felt something I hadn't experienced before—one sniff and I was transported to a dream life. The candle scent made me imagine myself living in Paris as an artist-entrepreneur with a gorgeous and spacious apartment. On my terrace, I would host sunset dinners with the best wine and delicious food made by my chef friends, all while light R&B music played in the background. It was all very specific. That candle was Au 17 by Maison Francis Kurkdjian. It has a luxuriously deep scent of incense, firewood, and warm amber. I thought there must have been some magic in that candle, because its fragrance made me feel something I had never felt before. Needless to say, I bought it, even though it was pricey (but I was in vacation mode, so why not?).

After I got home from that great trip, I went back to the daily grind. By 2019, the candle was a memory long gone, and I was deep in a rut of endless work. The more I worked, the less happy I was. I needed to make life beautiful again.

I was tidying up my small one-bedroom apartment one day and came across the candle that I had bought almost a year ago in Paris. I opened it up, took a whiff, and it happened again: The scent took over the moment. But this time, I was transported back to that incredible vacation. The magic of Paris with friends. I could feel it all. My whole energy changed. I had been looking for a new creative expression, and I thought, why not post about candles online and how they can make you feel? I could share how personal living with and loving candles could be. As someone who lives a very organized and regimented life, I wanted a space that was free, creative, and where I could be my most authentic self, sharing thoughts straight from my mind about how candles and scents brought joy to my life. I didn't think anyone would watch my videos in a serious way, so I just went for it. I decided to call the account "Sir Candle Man," and my first post was about that fateful Maison Francis Kurkdjian's Au 17 candle.

I didn't have a lot of followers for a few years. Honestly, I didn't care; I was posting about something I loved. I was feeling alive, rejuvenated, and inspired again, and I wanted other people to feel the same. With now over one hundred thousand followers on multiple platforms, I would never have imagined building such a vibrant community of fellow candle lovers and making friends with candle-brand owners, perfumers, and fragrance influencers, including, incredibly, meeting the Maison Francis Kurkdjian PR team. Mama, I had made it!

Meeting the PR team was a full-circle moment that I could never have dreamed of. The part that made that moment even more special is that when their team described the Au 17 candle to me, they spoke about how the candle was inspired by Francis Kurkdjian's own home—the scents he likes, how the black color inside of the vessel was inspired by the black-painted walls in his home, and how the gold lid is the specific gold that you see on the rooftops in Paris. When I first smelled this candle, it made me imagine myself living a whole life in Paris, and guess what? That's exactly the feeling the candle was meant to evoke. In that moment, it clicked: Fragrance is an art that helps make your life beautiful, and everyone deserves to feel that.

Sir Candle Man's mission was defined.

lessons from a love affair with candles

Since that fateful day in Paris in 2018, when my candle journey began, I have smelled and tried countless candles. I own hundreds of candles; I have gifted more candles that I can count.

My life has been enriched by the joy of candles and scent. I've been featured in many publications, attended the prestigious Fragrance Foundation Awards, made my own luxury candle collaboration, and now I am writing this book. Even though all these achievements have been so cool and gratifying, my love for candles is deeper than notoriety. Living with and loving candles has taught me so much about myself and about life, and I want you to have that too. Here are some lessons I've learned from my love affair with candles:

1 | YOU DESERVE BEAUTIFUL THINGS. I used to be scared to spend money on expensive candles, but after I did, my whole life changed. How your home or space smells is important because it can determine your

mood. You deserve the very best and you should not be scared to invest if you're able to.

2 | YOU CAN MAKE YOUR OWN LIFE BEAUTIFUL. I used to hope and wait for life to get better. Little did I know that embarking on this journey of finding and posting about the candles I loved would bring me so much joy. It's proof that building a life you love is right there in your hands. Find something you love and do it as often as you can.

3 | YOU DESERVE TO TAKE A BREAK. I used to rush through my days. I would wake up, get ready for work, drive, spend hours looking at a screen, hurry home, eat, work some more, and then crash into bed. When I started lighting candles, I had to stop, light the candle, smell the scent, and wait for it to fill the room. Candles forced me to be present, to enjoy taking a break, and to make moments for self-care. To thrive, you must also rest.

4 | YOU DESERVE SUCCESS. I used to think that success only came from grinding yourself down to almost nothing. But I have learned that success can also flow easily. Yes, I put in a lot of work as Sir Candle Man, but the work doesn't grind me down. The work actually fills me up. Talking about and sharing my love of candles feels so authentic, fun, and easy for me. My passion has brought me a lot in return. You can live a great life that you work for without feeling worn out.

Part I

Everything
You Need to

Know
about
Candles

getting lit

HOW TO SHOP FOR CANDLES

One of my favorite parts of living the candle lifestyle is shopping for them. After burning hundreds of candles, I have simplified what I look for in a candle to make my shopping experience fun and easy: scent, strength, style, and wax.

I have one key piece of advice before you start shopping, and that is not to get caught up in the price of the candles. When I first started building my collection, I used to think that higher prices meant that the candles were better and more luxurious. That could not be further from the truth. Candle prices are impacted by so many variables, from ingredients to vessel materials to branding, as well as supply chain issues and much more. There are plenty of great candles available at various price points, so buy what's in your budget and you'll be more than fine. There are $10, $30, and $150 candles I love. But more importantly, the choice is personal. Whether you spend a little or a lot, you're going to be burning it away anyway.

THE SCENT

Let's start by finding the perfect scent for you. The best scents tell a story or paint a picture in your mind. I went for my first big candle shopping trip a few years ago at a store called Candle Delirium in Los Angeles. I was fascinated to see thousands of different candles in just one store. So many wonderful, interesting, and strange scents. At first it was a little overwhelming, so I stuck to the notes I knew and loved, such as sandalwood, vanilla, teakwood, and cedarwood. After a while, one of the store managers came over and asked if I needed help. He said he would show me a variety of candles if I told him the scents I loved. I said that I like woody, deep, and uplifting scents. We sniffed a few candles, and then we got to LAFCO's Feu du Bois candle and my whole mood shifted. *Feu du bois* means "wood fire" or "burning wood" in French. And yes, it did have smoky and woody elements from the sandalwood, but what struck me is that the candle also goes by "Ski House," and that's what came to mind when I smelled it. It had a cozy, sitting-next-to-a-fire-with-a-vanilla-type-of-drink vibe with some spicy notes. As someone who has only skied once, I could feel myself nestling into the couch while looking at the snow outside.

This is the power of fragrance: It has the ability to transport you to different places or create vivid experiences in your mind. More than the scent, that feeling made me buy the candle immediately and it has become one of my top ten candles of all time. Now, I don't need every candle

to take me on a trip, but I do want a candle scent to stand out and enhance my life in a beautiful way. I believe in this concept so much that when I was collaborating with L'or de Seraphine on my first candle, I started the creative process by sharing the feeling and the story that I wanted people to experience when they lit the candle. I landed on the idea of creating a "soft life" for yourself that smells like a fresh peach Bellini under the shade of a majestic fig tree. A talented perfumer, Erwan Raguenes, at the fragrance house Firmenich, was able to build the fragrance, and it smelled exactly like that. I now know that building a special fragrance is an art form. From the fragrance houses to the perfumers to the technicians, it takes a team of skilled professionals to make a fragrance come alive. The work is both technical and creative. That is what you are paying for.

Fragrances are made up of notes that create accords (a group of materials making up a unique scent). Almost all perfumes have what is known as a "fragrance pyramid" with base notes, middle notes, and top notes.

Base notes are stable and foundational. Longer lasting with heavier, deeper notes, they often consist of notes like vanilla and amber, woods like sandalwood and cedarwood, and leather.

Middle notes are the heart of the fragrance, and these scents build on the base in a complementary or an interesting way. Think of notes like rose, neroli, cinnamon, and balsam fir, which can hold your attention.

Top notes are what you smell first when you open the candle. Don't be fooled by the top notes and imagine that they're what the candle will smell like when lit. What you're experiencing is the "cold throw" (see page 33). You can only truly know what a candle will smell like when it's lit and you've given it enough time to fill the room.

To help you get a better sense of the candle's scent while you're shopping, read the description on the packaging (if there is one). Now that you understand fragrance layers, the importance of storytelling in perfumery, and going with what you like, picture the perfect scent for you as if it were a painting: All the colors (scent notes) need to work together to create a beautiful painting (fragrance).

THE STRENGTH

After deciding which fragrances you like, you should consider how strong you want them to be. Most people love a strong candle fragrance because you get more bang for your buck. This scent formulation is called "the juice" in the industry. I love a medium-strength juice.

I test new candles all the time, and early on in my candle journey a new candle brand sent me their latest candle. The scent had a strong gardenia note. Gardenia is very distinct and fragrant—floral, green, zesty, and a little sweet. I've since come to appreciate the note, but back then, when I opened the box, I almost coughed and had to

REAL VS. SYNTHETIC SCENTS

Should you care about buying fragrances made using real or synthetic perfume ingredients? Fun fact: A lot of fragrances are made with synthetic ingredients because they are cheaper to produce while maintaining the quality. Sometimes it's more sustainable to make the fragrances synthetically, given the amount of raw material needed to produce the real version. So, overall, it doesn't really matter. If you are a purist, yes, you can get a candle that is made from pure ingredients like essential oils. But, ultimately, you should look for fragrances that smell great to you.

take a step back. I decided I should give it a try, because I hoped it would burn differently, but I was wrong. In the five minutes after I lit the candle, my whole apartment smelled like a garden filled with gardenias that I was trapped in against my will. The candle was so strong that I got a mild headache. I extinguished the flame and stored it away, but every time I passed by the storage area, I would smell the candle. I ended up giving it away. From that day on, I knew that I loved a medium-scented candle. For me, scent should be uplifting and soothing, not assaulting. (But if you like a strong candle, you do you!)

On the other hand, a scented candle can't be too light on the juice, because if the fragrance is too light, then what's the point? When I first started buying candles, I was worried about spending too much money on them, so I would try to find candles with scents similar to candles from popular luxury brands. These are known as "dupes." I once found an almost exact dupe for a gorgeous creamy sandalwood candle that I loved, and I was beyond excited to try it. The day came and I lit that baby up, and at first, the candle smelled amazing. But after an hour or so, I was struggling to smell anything. I searched online and found that many people had experienced the same thing. While the candle was a solid scent dupe, it did not have the power I wanted. In the end, I probably should have spent the money on the candle that had the strength that I wanted from the bigger brand. All of this is to say, spend the money on the right juice.

Take the time to find the right brand for you. Certain candle brands are known for having strong fragrances, while some are known for having lighter fragrances. As you shop more, you'll find the brands and scent strengths you gravitate toward. There is also a place for unscented candles, especially if you just want to create a relaxing vibe, but I'm such a fragrance lover that I almost always want some perfumery in my candles.

HOT AND COLD THROW

You don't need to stay lit to get lit! The often-not-spoken-about secret to filling your home with delicious scents is that you don't always have to light up your candle to get its sweet-smelling benefits. A candle's "throw" is how far the fragrance can travel in a space. Candles can smell different when they're lit. The "hot throw" is the fragrance strength and dispersion you get when the candle is lit. For a dinner party, I want a strong candle to fill the room, but at night, when I'm winding down, I want something light and soothing. "Cold throw" refers to the strength of a candle before it is lit. Sometimes you don't want open flames in rooms you don't enter often or in rooms you wouldn't think to light a candle in often (like a study), but you still want them to smell like home. The trick to this is to get a strong candle with signature base notes and put them in these rooms so that their fragrant cold throws fill the room every time you enter. You can also use the combination of hot and cold throws to create unique scents for your space.

THE STYLE

Once you have chosen your favorite scent and decided how strong you want your candle to be, you need to find the right vessel for it. Candles comes in many shapes and sizes, so you want to make sure the candle you pick fits right into your home and space.

When I first started buying candles on a regular basis, I would always pick candles in a clear glass vessel that was round with a simple and elegant label. But one day, my friend suggested I try Voluspa candles, which come in the most gorgeous, colorful, and ornate vessels—a home-decor dream. This was the first time I realized how much a great-looking vessel can elevate your candle game. Beautiful candles somehow smell better (if the fragrance is good, that is).

As I started learning about niche fragrance houses that made candles, I was introduced to brands that took the craftsmanship of building the vessel as seriously as the scent. You can find meticulously crafted iron vessels, intricately printed ceramic vessels, delicately embossed glass, and so many other options, especially with special edition candles from your favorite brands. To me, these candles are collector's items. And what's even better is that you can reuse the vessels for so many other things once the candle has burned out: pen holders, cotton-ball holders, accent pieces, drinking cups . . . the list is endless. I would encourage you to try lots of different styles. These styles will add dimension and fun to your home (see page 126 for how to style your candles).

Lastly, the size of the candle matters, but size is not everything (wink, wink). Choose a candle that fits the space you'll burn it in. Some people believe that the more wicks a candle has, the better. That is not true. You need the right number of wicks for the right size candle to make sure it burns evenly. I typically go for one wick and max out at three wicks, but I've seen candles with ten wicks and more. For candles that I end up loving a lot, I will buy them in different sizes so that I can put them in as many spaces in my home as possible, depending on the size of each room: a larger candle for my living room, a medium-size candle for my bedroom, and a small candle for my bathroom. If you find a signature scent, don't be shy—buy as many as you can within your budget.

THE WAX

Beyond the alchemy of the scent notes, there is one key ingredient that brings everything together and is often taken for granted: the wax. There are lots of different waxes to choose from, such as soy, beeswax, coconut wax, paraffin wax, and palm wax, to name a few, and there is much debate about which types of waxes are good and which are bad. I have tried candles made from many different waxes and wax blends, and I care most about the wax or wax blend that carries and burns the fragrance best and in a clean way.

What is a clean burn? A clean-burning candle does not create excess smoke when it burns and does not leave dark soot on the vessel or on your walls. A clean candle is also free of toxins. I like a candle that does not emit a chemical smell when I light it, which happens sometimes with paraffin-forward waxes (though you can find paraffin wax in many wax blends because it helps carry fragrance). The waxes that burn most cleanly are plant-based or natural: soy, coconut, palm, and beeswax.

I've learned so much about waxes over the past few years. One of my favorite candles is from Lola James Harper. When I asked the company why the candle smelled so amazing and burned so well, they introduced me to the world of wax makers and wax masters. Many high-end candle brands spend as much time working on their wax blends and the interaction between the fragrance and the wax as they do on the scent blend in order to produce the desired outcome and feeling of the candle. If the interaction goes awry, the scent might change, the wax might turn a weird color, and other problems might arise.

If you care about the type of wax you are buying, you should check the wax type on the packaging or look it up on the brand's website. Some waxes are less expensive, which allows brands to make the candle at a more accessible price for everyone, and some waxes help project more fragrance at the expense of the cleanliness of the burn. I went through a "clean era," where I only wanted candles made from natural ingredients, so I purchased some pure soy and beeswax candles. They smelled amazing, but some of the candles started turning different colors after several burns. This can happen from time to time, so if you care how your candles look in your home, this may not work for you. Check out the reviews and decide what is best for you.

BUILDING YOUR STARTER CANDLE COLLECTION

After trying many candles over the years, I believe that every home needs these four types:

1. A DAILY SIGNATURE CANDLE

2. A RELAXING CANDLE

3. A REFRESHING AND ENERGIZING CANDLE

4. A BOUGIE LUXURY CANDLE

My early candle days were filled with deep woody, leathery, smoky, and whiskey notes. People tend to call these masculine notes, even though fragrance truly has no gender. Looking back, I probably bought candles with those notes because of social conditioning about what a man should like, especially a Black man. I was too scared to lean into all the scents I liked, such as rose, green leafy notes, citrus, and even vanilla. Over time, I let go of the idea of scent being gendered and then I was able to enjoy candles so much more.

Moral of the story? Don't let other people's opinions and expectations dictate what you like.

SOMETHING SIGNATURE

Have you noticed how some places always smell so good? Hotel lobbies, certain friends' homes, luxury spas, and boutiques, for example. I believe every home should smell amazing as well. And with the right candle, you can make that happen.

I once visited a famous celebrity's home for a meeting. I was just so giddy to be there. The home was massive and beautiful with incredible art and gorgeous home decor. As I was working my way through the meeting agenda, I kept being distracted by a delicate scent in the air. The fragrance in the home was exquisite—I had never smelled anything like it before. We wrapped up the meeting and then I looked around quickly and saw that they had a Le Labo Santal candle burning in the corner. On the way out, I noticed that this candle was everywhere in the house. This was their signature scent. The creamy sandalwood goodness was all over the home, and it created a safe "scent bubble" that I didn't want to leave. From that day onward, I made it a priority to have my own signature candle for my home.

My first signature candle scent was a vanilla bourbon candle. I still remember it to this day, because it reminds me of when I was starting a big new job—the smell of sweet excitement. As much as I loved it, I got over that smell quickly because it was too sweet and too strong. But over time, I've come to like gentle floral and woody notes

for my home. This combination feels grounded but delicate and slightly sweet, which makes for an inoffensive and always pleasurable experience.

Your signature candle should make anyone who enters you home say, "Oh my goodness, it smells so good in here." This scent is the foundation of your space. Ideally, your signature scent should have notes that feel like a warm embrace or bring you a sense of grounding. I like sandalwood, amber, and vanilla, or, even better, a warm vanilla-wood combination of all three. Other options are clean linen or a light floral. Overall, a home should always feel sweet and inviting, literally "home sweet home" in a fragrance.

Wood, vanilla, clean linen, and amber all make for terrific signature home scents.

SOMETHING RELAXING

There is nothing quite like the experience of walking into a luxury spa. The combination of citrus notes, fresh green notes, aquatic elements, and touches of floral almost always instantly relax me as soon as I enter the space. Everyone deserves to be able to bring this feeling to life in their home, and a candle is a great way to do that.

I once went on a trip to Istanbul for work. My days were filled with work, meetings, and evening events. I enjoyed seeing the sights, tasting the food, and making new friends, but after a few days I was tired and decided to book some spa treatments for my last day in the city. In Turkey, they have traditional spas called hammams, where the massages are amazing. You get a full body scrub followed by a light foam massage, and you feel squeaky clean afterward. I wanted a luxurious version of the massage, so I booked it at a great hotel. While the massage was amazing, what struck me the most was the scent of the space and, more specifically, the resting area I relaxed in after the massage. The fragrance in the room was calming, reinvigorating, and sweet at the same time. I probably laid there longer than I needed to because of that gorgeous smell. To this day, I dream about capturing that smell in a candle.

The "something relaxing" candle should feel like a deep exhale after a tough day. That feeling you get as you release the top button, take off your tight tie, and put on your home clothes. I like lavender, the freshness of petitgrain, and, if you're feeling fun, the smell of green tea—it works really well. Clary sage is an ideal note for a grounding feeling. Candles with these relaxing notes can be burned right when you get back home or when you are winding down to get ready for bed and a deep restorative sleep (see page 110 for more candle rituals).

Citrus, green, and aquatic scents are perfect for relaxing.

SOMETHING FRESH

Sometimes you need a pick-me-up to get you over a hump in the day, or you need a candle for an invigorating Saturday-morning cleaning session. This is where fresh and zesty candles shine. Eucalyptus, citrus, or herbal notes like rosemary will do the trick and you'll be feeling the pep in your step again in no time.

On any given weekend morning, I will wake up, open all the windows to let the air and light in, pour myself a strong cup of coffee, light some uplifting candles in all the rooms, turn on my favorite R&B playlist, call my family, read a little, then get to cleaning up to restore my home to a peaceful place. I like lighting a citrus or fresh herbal candle when I'm ready to clean. The feeling of having a home that is clean, smells good, and filled with great music is unparalleled.

When I am really feeling down and need a fast pick-me-up, I light a single-note herbal candle like eucalyptus, thyme, rosemary, petitgrain, orange blossom, or lemon. These candles are the perfect way to instantly cut through the tension of your home and shift the energy. This is an excellent way to bring your attention back into focus on the present moment and help you get past any procrastination, laziness, or humps you may be feeling.

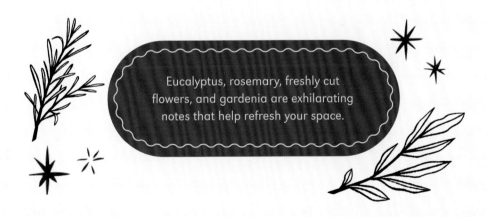

Eucalyptus, rosemary, freshly cut flowers, and gardenia are exhilarating notes that help refresh your space.

SOMETHING BOUGIE

Bougie means "candle" in French, so it's natural that treating yourself to a luxury candle exemplifies what I like to call "bougie for no reason" energy.

Every now and then, you have to treat yourself to something special. Your days can be stressful and life can seem a bit much, so why not buy yourself something nice? This is where luxury candles come in. The super-luxury candle is the candle you take out for a fancy occasion or when you want to elevate your mood and make yourself feel taken care of.

For my birthday a few years ago, two friends bought me some very nice candles. I was used to spending up to $50 or $60 on a candle, but when I checked the prices of my gifted candles I was shocked. At the time, I was new to luxury fragrance, and I had no idea that candles could go for hundreds of dollars. As someone who had to learn to accept abundance in their life, I was too scared to light those candles and embarrassed to show them in my videos. Eventually I got over it and posted them. As expected, there was a little bit of a backlash about why anyone would spend that much money on a candle. I was also positively surprised to see how many people either had the candles or were interested in saving up to buy the candles. Out of curiosity, I asked these folks why they would spend that much money on a candle, and the reasons were almost always the same: the joy of owning something luxurious or retail therapy. There is no one expensive product that will make your whole life better, but it feels good to save up to buy something for the sole purpose of spoiling yourself. Being okay with spending money on yourself is a beautiful act of self-love. Just make sure you stay within your life budget—you don't want to wind up broke from buying candles.

BOUGIE

Some luxury brands that I love on the expensive side are Carrière Frères, Trudon, LAFCO, diptyque, and Maison Francis Kurkdjian. In the mid-range I like NEST New York, Boy Smells, Otherland, Apotheke, and Harlem Candle Company. And in a slightly more affordable price range, I like P.F. Candle Co., 228 Grant Street Candle Co., and Simply Curated.

There are many reasons luxury candles are so expensive, including branding, ingredients, history, and craftsman-ship. Luxury houses like Tom Ford produce candles that smell lovely packaged in exquisite vessels that make for great decor. Fragrance houses like Trudon are among the first candle makers, so you're paying for their heritage, skill, and solid luxury vessels. Some brands use only the finest and rarest ingredients to create unique fragrances that are expensive to make, so the candle is priced accordingly. Paying for quality is acceptable to me, but do your research and learn about the brand before spending a lot of money.

I also like my expensive candles to look expensive. I know that some people prefer understated luxury, which I totally understand, but if I am buying an expensive candle, I want my inner bougieness to shine. I want the candle to look incredible—maybe with some gold on the vessel, black wax, or handblown glass. Whatever it is, it must scream luxury.

I also want my candle scents to smell expensive. Notes that I find deeply luxurious are leather, plum, bourbon, and smoke. That combination is how I would imagine a secret high-end jazz bar to smell: an intoxicating combination of expensive perfumes, the finest cigars, and delicious cocktails.

Spend some money on yourself—you deserve it.

LET'S ACCESSORIZE

By now, you should know how to select a candle with the right scent, strength, style, and wax. What do we have left? Everything else that comes with the candle lifestyle: the accessories.

Matches and Lighters

I used to only use matches to light my candles and then blow them out when I was done, but I now know that blowing out candles is not the best way to extinguish the flame (see page 64). Matches are good, and I've also seen so many beautiful types—long ones, colorful ones, interestingly packaged ones. Add distinctive boxes of matches to your candle kit for some extra flair. You can also get electric rechargeable lighters that come in cool colors like rose gold if you want to color coordinate them with the decor of your space.

Wick Trimmers, Dippers, and Snuffers

In addition to matches, you can buy accessories like wick trimmers, wick dippers, and wick snuffers to elevate your candle-burning experience. Lighting a candle requires using a basic technique (refer to page 59), and trimming your wick to the right length is critical. You could use a pair of scissors, but I like using a beautiful wick trimmer. I have one in gold and one in black, and I hope to design one in the future. Similarly, putting out a candle, outside of blowing out the flame, can also be done better using a wick dipper or a snuffer. I have seen some ornately engraved tools that enhance the experience as well as serve as easy decor for your home.

Cloches and Hurricanes

The biggest discovery I made about myself over years of collecting and lighting candles is how much I enjoy home decor. I once found myself in one of those bougie and highly curated home-decor stores, and I noticed they had a candle section where all the candles were nicely lined up in a row under clear glass cloches. The arrangement was so clean and pretty—it made me feel happy. Cloches are attractive and functional because they provide a gorgeous, streamlined aesthetic, and they also hold some of the fragrance by covering the candle. They also give you a sneak peek of what the candle smells like before you light it—I use cloches as a way to test fragrances before I light them. One day I

want to have a big candle-library room full of candles under cloches with neat labels underneath, but for now, I'll settle for a few cloches in my apartment. A glass hurricane candle holder, which is open at the top, is another elegant way to display a candle, but it will not protect the candle from dust.

Trays

When I was decorating the second apartment I moved into in Los Angeles, I hired a virtual interior decorator to help me make my space feel grown-up, elegant, and put together. I had told her that I had a lot of candles that I wanted to place in my space in beautiful and interesting ways, and when she made her recommendations, I was initially surprised at how many trays and hurricanes she suggested that I buy. Who needed that many trays? Turns out she knew what was up! Trays are your friend—they come in different sizes, colors, and textures—because they can make any surface appear well organized while looking intentionally and sleekly designed. Do yourself a favor and buy beautiful trays to wrangle the loose items in your home—you won't regret it.

WHERE TO FIND THE BEST CANDLES FOR LESS

I love shopping for candles at different price ranges, but I also love a good deal just as much as anyone else, so I shop in a number of places, both online and in person, to find the best offers.

- **CANDLE-BRAND WEBSITES:** These sites typically have a first-time customer discount, so I always check for a discount code before checkout.

- **BEAUTY RETAILERS:** Try to shop during their seasonal sales, or keep an eye out for when specific brands do a general sale or markdowns.

- **RESELLERS:** You can find good prices through resellers, but I tend not to shop from these vendors as it's difficult to confirm the authenticity of the product. I know people who buy from resellers often, but it's a risk you should be aware of.

- **DEPARTMENT STORES:** Many big stores that sell fine fragrances (perfume) also sell candles. Walk around and be on the lookout for any perfume bundles that may have a candle in the deal.

- **SPECIALTY CANDLE STORES:** These places primarily sell candles (shout-out to Candle Delirium in West Hollywood). You can have so much fun at these stores, because they have deep candle selections.

- **BOUTIQUES AND FARMERS MARKETS:** Shopping at smaller stores helps support local small businesses, and they may have unique finds based on their personal relationships with candle-brand owners.

CANDLE CARE 101

If you take care of your candles, they will take care of you. From setting up the burn, the actual burn, and ending the burn, there is a sequence to the ritual.

A few years ago, a friend bought me a luxury candle as a gift. I used to light it for only a few minutes a day to savor the smell without using up too much of it because I wanted it to last forever. But after a few burns, I noticed that it was burning inward and creating a deep hole in the middle of the vessel, leaving a lot of unburned wax on the sides of the candle, known as "tunneling." It was a rookie mistake, and my beloved candle was ruined.

I now know that tunneling can easily be fixed if it's caught early enough (see page 62), but because I had done this for so long, I couldn't recover this candle. In this section, you'll find everything you need to know about lighting and burning candles so that you don't make the same mistake. Here are five steps for burning your candle right every time.

STEP ONE

The wick. Trim that thang.

This is the most important step in the pre-lighting ritual.
I've now lit thousands of candles, and to this day, I make
sure that I do this step every time I open a new one. You
should trim the wick to a quarter inch before every burn
(yes, every burn!), from the first time you light a new candle
and every burn after that. You may have noticed that some
wicks are extra long when you first open the candle, and
it's especially important to trim those down. I've always
wondered why the manufacturer doesn't trim the wick to
the right length in the first place, but hey, here we are.

There are several reasons to cut the wick to a quarter inch.

- The longer the wick, the bigger the flame, causing
  your candle to burn faster and causing you to miss
  out on more hours of candle joy.

- A flame that's too hot may alter and neg-
  atively affect how the fragrance burns;
  you don't want to lose the juice simply
  because you didn't trim the wick.

- Lastly, if you are relighting a candle
  that has a burnt wick, that will create
  more smoke when it burns, and
  more soot will accumulate in

the vessel. You want a clean and even burn, so trust me, trim that wick.

For me, enjoying candles is a lifestyle, so I keep dedicated wick trimmers on hand because they're an important part of my candle-lighting ritual. Also, they're a little bougie, they can be used as decor, and they make you feel chic. You can get yourself a pair of inexpensive, and beautiful, wick trimmers online. But to be honest, you don't need to buy a wick trimmer—anything that can trim works, including a pair of scissors you probably already have.

STEP TWO

Light. Do it right.

When you light your candle, you have to light it for the right amount of time. You want to build up what is called "candle memory": The candle remembers up to what point you lit it the last time, and that's how far it's going to go the next time you burn it (almost like that space in your bed that molded to the shape of your body). That luxury candle I mentioned earlier could have been saved had I done this step correctly. Because I was so protective of my beautiful candle and didn't want to use too much of it, I was lighting it for too short a time, which caused the tunnel in the middle.

The key is to burn your candle long enough to have a full melt pool on top. This means making sure that the top

layer of the wax melts all the way to the edge of the vessel on every burn. Yes, on every single burn. A full melt pool will ensure that when you burn the candle again, because of candle memory, it will burn evenly down the sides of the vessel without tunneling.

How long does it take to get to a fully melted wax pool? Well, you'll need a lot of patience. Candles are not to be rushed. I would urge you to enjoy the process and enjoy the burn. For a regular-size nine-ounce candle, a full melt pool could take two to three hours. I try to use my candles during meditative moments or tasks that I know will take time, such as cleaning, cooking, reading, journaling, watching TV shows, or writing. I'm burning a candle as I write this book right now. I understand that you may want to save your beautiful candles by burning them for a few minutes at a time, but I urge you to commit and let them burn. There is an abundance of beautiful candles out in the world for you, so just go all in. You should use and enjoy all your nice things, because you deserve them, and you should know that more will come your way and light up your life.

STEP THREE
Placement. Stay still.

Where you place your candle matters. I once moved into an apartment the day after it was repainted and the fumes from the paint were still very fresh and overwhelming.

FIXING A TUNNELED CANDLE

Sometimes things go wrong. Even if you are lighting your candle correctly, it may still tunnel. Not to worry, this can be fixed if you catch it early, before the tunnel is too deep. A little aluminum foil and patience will do the trick. The first thing to do is to trim your wick to a quarter inch. Then light the candle and put some aluminum foil around it while leaving a little hole at the top for the hot air to escape through. This DIY heater will create enough directed heat to melt the wax around the edges of the vessel and help it even out with the rest of the wax. This method works like a charm almost every time. Some people use a blowtorch to melt the sides of the wax that way, but that approach scares me because I'm a little clumsy and I don't want to create a fiery situation in my home.

I appreciated the new coat, but breathing that paint-infused air was rough, so I drove to my local home-goods store and picked up two big and strong candles to help re-scent the space. I still remember the vanilla, cognac, and tobacco scent to this day—delicious!

While the fragrance was incredible, I made a grave mistake that I will never make again: I placed my candle close to a fan and a window. I was trying to use the ventilation to waft into the space faster, but instead, I ended up with candle vessels that had soot on the inside, and worse, I noticed some soot on the ceiling and walls. The movement of air plus an untrimmed wick (I had not learned my lesson yet) led to soot being blown into the room and up to the ceiling. If you have tried to clean soot off a ceiling, you know it's really messy and goes everywhere.

The key is to place your candle away from any area that has a draft or a breeze, like a window or fan, or an air vent. Candles like being stable, and a draft moves the flame around, which will in turn make your candle burn unevenly, and if the wick is too long, an uneven burn will create soot that can be blown into your home. If your goal is to have more fragrance in your home, instead of trying my failed hack, buy yourself candles with stronger throws (more on that on page 33) or bigger candles with more wicks, and let the candles do their thing.

STEP FOUR

Stop. Easy does it.

I think a lot about birthday cakes and how we blow out the candles. When I was young, this seemed fun, but now that I'm older I think about the germs a lot. How is this related to scented candles? It came to mind because I used to put out candles in the same way—by blowing out the flame. When you do this, you end up with a little bit of smoke, which I don't mind, but I know a lot of people do. Blowing out a candle directly is not entirely wrong or the worst thing you can do, but there are other ways to extinguish the flame that are fun, chic, and a little bougie and leave you with minimal to no smoke at all.

The best way to put out a candle with almost no smoke is to use a wick dipper, or, for longer candles like tapers, to use a wick snuffer (more on candle accessories on page 52). A wick dipper allows you to easily dip the burning wick into the melted wax, immediately putting out the flame. Even better, this contraption coats the wick with a little wax, which helps give you a cleaner burn the next time you light the candle. The wick snuffer is placed over the flame, limiting the oxygen and thus extinguishing the candle. Wick trimmers and snuffers are not must-have items, but they are definitely nice to have and make for interesting decorative accents. More importantly for me, they help create a ritual around candles, which can add beauty to your life and contribute to self-care routines. I'll say it again: You deserve beautiful things!

STEP FIVE

Store. Keep cool.

My candle collection and I have lived in many apartments. In the summer of 2020, I moved into a gorgeous, bright, and airy apartment because I needed a change from the dreary place I was living and working in after the pandemic forced me to work from home. I decided to buy myself a beautiful shelf on which to place and store my candles in a decorative way. That summer was very hot, and while I had air-conditioning, it was no match for the extreme heat we were experiencing. One day, I was reorganizing my candles when I noticed that some of them were forming little oil spots on top. The candles were sweating. Some of the candles also had dust on the top layer of wax, which was concerning. I smelled one of my favorites and the aroma was terrible. Something had changed, and I wasn't quite sure what it was. I now know that if you don't store your candles correctly, they will deteriorate quickly. The scent and the look of the candle may change for the worse.

Store your candles in a cool, dry place. If candles are stored or displayed in hot places, the color of the wax may change, they will sweat, and the strength of the fragrance

PROTECT YOUR INNER FLAME

I light a lot of candles in my life—you would think I'd be over it by now. But I'm not. And there is one lesson of living the candle life that I turn to often, and it's that you can't make a candle burn faster than it wants to. You must pause, decide what scent you want, prepare the candle, light it, and wait for it to burn. Then, you must pause again and remember to put it out. Nowadays, people rarely stop. We're running from one thing to the next, scrolling on our phones, switching from tab to tab. Worrying about one thing or another. Taking the time to light a candle is like a ritual. A moment of self-care. A moment to treat yourself. Just as you'd take good care of your favorite candle, don't forget to care for the inner flame of the amazing person you are. Protect that at all costs.

will be reduced. Some candles come with lids, which is beneficial because the lid prevents dust and small debris (and even little bugs) from getting into the wax, which will ensure that your candle continues to smell great and burn well. If your candle doesn't have a lid, store it in a drawer or cabinet—just make sure it's away from heat and moisture.

After paying lots of money for luxury candles, the last thing you want is for the juice to be messed up or for your candle to look wonky. Store your candles correctly and they will burn well for a long time.

SHARING THE LOVE WITH CANDLE GIFTS

I've collected a number of candles over the years. To be honest, I keep a lot of them for myself, but I also really like to give candles to my friends and family. Whenever a friend is over, I let them take a candle or two. They leave so happy and excited about lighting the candles, which truly brings me so much joy. I'm most excited that they will enjoy the magic of fragrance, light up their home with the scent, and tell me how it makes them feel.

Why are candles the perfect gift? They are beautiful, uplifting, affordable, and luxurious. Gifts should be memorable, and scent helps lock memories in place. Whether you go affordable or go all out, helping someone make their home and life smell even more beautiful is thoughtful, kind, and, honestly, very cool. Every time someone lights a candle you gave them, they will think of you. Here are some of my tried-and-true tips for gifting a candle that makes a mark.

IT'S ALL IN THE SCENT

There are some ground rules to keep in mind when giving someone a candle, because your gesture might backfire if you pick the wrong candle or give the wrong scent to the recipient. When in doubt, play it safe: Choose a generally loved scent profile. Most people love anything that "smells good," so try picking a candle with notes of wood, vanilla, or light florals. If you want to branch out, here are some of my favorite candle scents and notes to give for specific occasions.

MOVING INTO A NEW HOME

A new home needs a new smell, especially if the new home has been repainted or renovated and you can still smell the paint or other building materials. You want to choose something with a slight sweetness, like vanilla or amber, that makes a home feel inviting, lived in, and comfortable, but is not so distinct that you would notice it every time you step into the house.

> TOP PICKS: *LAFCO Amber Black Vanilla, L'or de Seraphine Monroe, Bastide Ambre Soir, and diptyque Vanille*

CELEBRATIONS, BIRTHDAYS, AND PROMOTIONS

I love gifting candles for big life moments in lieu of a more expected (and fleeting) gift like champagne or flowers. If you know the person well, this is a good time to choose a candle that has a name that matches the person or the occasion. There are a lot of brands online that produce candles with fun names that make for the perfect gift. Just make sure that the candle smells good—don't let a good name and good branding persuade you to buy a candle with a bad scent.

> TOP PICKS: *Voluspa Sparkling Cuvée, LAFCO Champagne, L'or de Seraphine Rêverie, Trudon Spella, and anything beautiful from Otherland*

PARTY FAVORS

Every good party has a charming takeaway for the guests. My goal is not to pressure people into spending more money to give a gift to people who came to your party, but I (almost) promise you that if you send your guests off with a great candle, it will make a mark and they will remember it. They will either burn the candle themselves or gift it to someone else. Scent is very personal, so I don't mind if someone regifts my candle. Ultimately, you've helped them out, so everybody wins. I find that sandalwood, light floral, vanilla, and citrusy candles are almost always well received. You want to go for universally loved notes.

TOP PICKS: *P.F. Candle Co.'s Teakwood & Tobacco, Le Labo's Santal 26, any FORVR Mood candle, Carrière Frères Tomato*

PARENTS AND FAMILY

I like to buy my family members candles to expose my loved ones to new scents. For instance, I like to share less traditionally masculine scents with my dad and less traditionally feminine scents with my mom. Scent is universal and should be enjoyed by everyone regardless of gender.

TOP PICKS: *Boy Smells Cameo (for the rose), Carrière Frères Robinia, and diptyque Figuier*

FOR NO REASON!

One of my favorite things to do is to surprise my friends with a candle gift. If they have shared their mailing address with me, I might send a candle through the mail to let them know that I am thinking of them. To me, fragrance is love, and I want to share it with those nearest and dearest to me. Every time they light the candle, they will think of you. Try to pick something they love if you know what scents they're fond of. Otherwise, stick to a more universally loved scent.

TOP PICKS: *Wickers Creek's gorgeous vessels, anything from Trudon is special, Mad et Len is a luxurious experience, Maison Margiela's Replica collection smells amazing, and Maison Francis Kurkdjian is top tier*

CONSIDER THE PERSON YOU'RE GIVING THE CANDLE TO

It's important to keep in mind that some people are allergic to perfumes and some people have pets that are sensitive to smells, so a scented candle may not always be the best gift. There are plenty of unscented or lightly scented candles that are beautiful too.

If you're concerned about choosing the wrong candle, opt for a gift card from a candle purveyor you like instead. I prefer to buy a gift card directly from a candle brand's website rather than from a generic retailer. Some might say this is forcing people to enjoy candles, but that's exactly the point!

ACCESSORIZE AND PERSONALIZE

To really amp up your gift game, you can include some accessories, such as wick trimmers, lighters, wick dippers, and more (see page 52 on candle accessories), in the gift package or gift basket. You can even get candles with funny names to match the personality of the person you are giving the candle to. You can have candles engraved with messages, names, or initials for an additional personal touch. Ultimately, think of the candle and the scent as the base of the gift and build around it to create something special and unique for the recipient. Sharing fragrance is like sharing your feelings: It's personal and it establishes a connection. Have fun with it!

A MEMORABLE GIFT

For my birthday a few years ago, my friend Stephanie bought me a Louis Vuitton candle. I was shocked—she's a very luxurious person, but I didn't expect her—or anyone else—to spend that much money on me. I love buying gifts for people, but I never expect to receive them. The luxury brand and the price really took me aback. I was so grateful that someone took the time to give me something that they knew I would love and, most of all, the fragrance was incredible. Thank goodness, because as you know by now, I really prioritize the fragrance over the price. From that day on, I leveled up my candle-gifting game. I still have that candle, and every time I look at it, I feel so happy and I'm reminded of Stephanie, our friend-ship, and her amazing gesture. That candle is in the center of my coffee table and has become part of my decor.

Part II

Bringing
Candle Love

into Your
Everyday Life

light up your life

CANDLES FOR THE VIBES

The power of scent is incredible: for memory, for comfort, for making your space your own. And just like with decor, scent sets the tone for your home. I believe that a house is not fully a home unless it smells amazing. Candles are the perfect way to create a magical experience for yourself and for your guests. Whether you want to relax, have fun with friends at a dinner party, or find the right scent to help you focus and get some work done, candles are the easiest way to change up a vibe almost instantly. There are so many things that could happen to you when you step outside your home, from rough workdays to stressful interactions, that when you step into your home you should have the power to change any negative frequency back to peace and positivity. Our homes are our sanctuaries, and the smell of a beautiful candle is an ideal way to make your sanctuary feel better. The following scents are some of my favorites for creating different vibes in your home.

THE "SMELLS SO GOOD" EVERY TIME YOU WALK IN VIBE

I associate my home with a signature scent (see page 42), and I think it's important to be intentional about how you make your home smell. Every time you step into your home, it should smell so good that you say, "Oh my goodness, I am so happy to be here." There are so many scents that are perfect for everyday enjoyment, but a good rule of thumb is to look for scents that are not too sharp, too strong, or too stringent. A great "welcome home" scent is one that's not too closely associated with a specific time of year or season, but is a scent that is lovable all year-round. And the best scents are those that evoke specific feelings or special memories for you.

Growing up, I spent a lot of time in my mother's flower shop, and while I was allergic to pollen and found myself sniffling all the time, I did love the smell of her shop, and in particular the fresh and sometimes piny scent of greenery accented with the sweet floral notes. That scent from the flower shop is a core memory for me—it gives me the feeling of comfort, of peace, of family, and of relaxation, and that's how I want my home to feel.

SCENT NOTES

My perfect "welcome home" notes are grounding scents: sandalwood, a good vanilla, stone fruit, cedarwood, vetiver. People will compliment these scents time and time again.

A key to creating the perfect signature scent is to make sure that you don't have too many strong scents in the room. Unless you're a pro "scent layerer" (see page 107), pick one great scent and let it lay the foundation of your scentscape. Here are a few notes to look for when curating your home's signature scent:

- FIG, which can transport you to the Mediterranean or a stroll in Paris. There is something mesmerizing about the green, milky, cool, slightly sweet combination that reminds me of a refreshing green smoothie at the start of the day.

- STONE FRUIT, which is a little bit sweet and a little bit juicy and smells like the moment just before you sip a fizzy summery cocktail.

- VETIVER is grounding, earthy, damp, and green— that special smell you find in luxury hotel bathroom soap that leaves you smelling your hands for the rest of the afternoon.

- VANILLA and SANDALWOOD, in combination, is creamy, warm, comforting, and sweet, like entering a farmhouse bakery where you want to buy all the treats.

- CEDARWOOD, a resin, camphor, and woody combination, is so soothing—it feels like exhaling after a day of holding your breath.

PLACEMENT

Placement is key to ensuring you get the perfect whiff as soon as you open the door. I like putting my core signature smell candles in the entryway to provide a warm invitation in, but you could also put your candle on a side table next to the couch or a seat that you sit in the most as a grounding reminder that you are home. Treat lighting this candle like a self-care ritual. A trick I like is to store my extra signature candles in my linen closet so that the scent infuses into my towels and sheets, enveloping me in fragrance in all aspects of my home life.

SWEET SOLO TIME

We all deserve moments of sweet solitude, and candles can provide the perfect scent backdrop to these moments—when you're resting, meditating, reading, journaling, or just spending some time chilling on the couch watching TV. There are many scents that cultivate a relaxing and healing atmosphere. I recommend scents that are grounding, have an earthy feeling, and are not so bold as to distract you from your moment of respite.

(See more about candles and wellness on page 110.)

Similar to most people, I live a pretty busy life. From my day job to my online life as Sir Candle Man—where I film multiple videos a week—to trying to maintain my relationships with family and friends, I find myself overwhelmed and stressed out a lot, and fragrance is a great way for me to unwind. Some days, I'll take a break and go for a walk. Luckily, I live in Los Angeles, where it's almost always sunny and warm, so the sun combined with the trees in my neighborhood have led me to love the very specific early, sunny, and grounding smell that I find when I'm taking a walk in the morning, and I own candles that evoke this scent. I love this smell so much that before filming videos to post online, I will light up a candle to center and ground my energy before I turn on the camera and press the RECORD button. These scents are like instant internal reboots for my system.

SCENT NOTES

I believe that relaxing scents need to have grounding energy. I love to use sage, palo santo, and lavender notes to achieve this energy. The scent should be medium to strong in nature, but not cloying or overpowering, meaning that every breath should feel restorative and not overwhelming. Here are some perfect solo-time notes:

- CLARY SAGE is the smell of sunshine and sweet dirt. It's like taking a hike on a summer day just before the sun gets too hot. It feels like the moment when you put your bare feet on the ground to reconnect and realign with nature.

- PALO SANTO is a subtly sweet, woody, and even a touch-bit-minty delicate fragrance that smells like rejuvenation—like going away to a silent retreat for a week and returning feeling better than ever.

- LAVENDER is the smell of Grandma's beautiful garden; it feels like a comforting, soothing, and reassuring hug.

PLACEMENT

For solo time, I like to place my candles in the center of the room I'm in to ensure that the whole room is filled with a grounding scent. Given the intentionality of this type of experience, being closer to the candle is a good thing for me.

GRIND TIME

There are times throughout the day when I need to focus deeply and get my work done. I love using scent to help create a space that's conducive to working and concentrating. More and more people are working from home these days and need a space that allows them to lock into the zone and get everything done. Scent can make work pleasurable. The key is to have something fresh but not too overpowering to help you maintain your focus.

In 2020, after the COVID-19 pandemic started, I was working from home and I had to make my cluttered apartment my workspace. My workdays are hectic, filled with meetings, pockets of deep-focus work, and times when major decisions need to be made. I tried my best to create dedicated spaces to work from, but even so, my apartment still felt super confined. I needed to find another way to help me relax and focus. Enter my beloved candles. On a regular day, I chose a small candle that I could burn right by my desk with a scent that wasn't so strong that it would distract me. I like notes of cedarwood or water lily for this. Sometimes I don't even light the candle but rather just take a whiff of the cold throw at my desk—that can be enough to relax my mind. On particularly stressful days with back-to-back video-call meetings, I light up the room with a soothing rosemary and eucalyptus candle from LAFCO to re-center myself, refresh my mind, and achieve Zen-like focus to power through. On a more relaxed day, like a Friday when I am clearing emails and finishing up projects, I choose scents that transport me to my favorite bustling coffee shop: aromas of coffee and sweet syrups to help lighten up the mood. That is the power of candles: They can transport you to any place or setting you want with their scent.

SCENT NOTES

If you want to have a candle on your desk, try to pick something with a medium throw or even a weak throw. A strong scent will overpower your senses and tempt you to focus on the scent and not the work, and we don't want distractions. With the right scents, you get to both de-stress from the daily pressure of work and also focus. Here are some great notes:

- WATER LILY or LAVENDER can be casual and calming, especially when working on complex or challenging problems.

- ROSEMARY, THYME, or EUCALYPTUS scents are refreshing and reinvigorating. These scents feel like a quick stop at your favorite luxury spa and just what you need to get energized to keep going.

For people with bigger spaces, like offices, you get to play even more. Choose a focus scent that is bold but welcoming, inviting but not overpowering:

- VANILLA is great for a larger space. It gets a bad rap because there are so many synthetic vanilla scents that are either too sweet or too "fake smelling," but with the right combination with a good vanilla, the scent can be magical (think vanilla and tobacco, vanilla and leather, vanilla and amber).

PLACEMENT

For grind time, either have a small candle on your desk that you light now and then, or burn a candle in the general work area of your office.

AFTER-WORK
UNWINDING

There is a very special time between the end of the workday and getting ready for bed after dinner. This is a time of unwinding, releasing the challenges of the day, being hopeful for a better day the next day, and dozing off to sleep. I, like many people, experience difficult workdays from time to time. Maybe you were challenged by your boss, asked to solve a complex problem that you didn't feel you could do, given some tough feedback, or bored by the day's tasks. Either way, when you open that door, kick your shoes off, and change into your home clothes, you have that exhale moment and the unwinding starts.

I like to be intentional about my unwinding process, and one way I bring myself back to the center is by immediately lighting a candle. The scent needs to be one that is joyful, one that can pull me into chill mode without making me sleepy. For me, the perfect unwinding notes are berries or rose. I find berry scents such as goji berry, currant, or even raspberry to be perfect just as long as they are not too sweet. The slightly sweet, juicy, and sparkling smell is always what I need after a less-than-amazing day. I light my candle, pour myself a glass of wine (or sometimes even champagne, because why not?), and dance to my favorite tunes for a few minutes—and all is right with the world again.

A few years ago, after months of considering and then purchasing diptyque's popular Baies candle, it finally arrived. I opened the box after a particularly stressful day at work. Excited to try this cult-favorite candle, I lit it, let it burn, poured myself a glass of wine, changed into my comfortable sweatpants, pressed PLAY on my favorite playlist, and settled in for the night. To this day, I still remember the first impression of the bursting sweetness of the candle's berry notes mixed with my favorite pop tunes in the background. It was magical.

SCENT NOTES

The best scents to help counteract a challenging day are ones that are uplifting and joyful. Here are some notes I like:

- BERRIES like GOJI BERRY, RED CURRANT, or RASPBERRY smell like the moment you put on your favorite upbeat record—like those first few bumps of the beat that send your serotonin levels up.

- ROSE smells exactly like walking through a well-manicured rose garden on a vacation in Europe: sweet, hopeful, and free. The perfect antidote to the stresses of the world.

- SWEET CITRUS, like TANGERINE, reinvigorates you with the effervescence and brightness in its scents. It's the perfect pick-me-up.

PLACEMENT

You can place these candles anywhere and everywhere. When lighting a candle to uplift your mood, more is more. In your living room, dining room, bathroom, bedroom—light it up where you need it!

DATE NIGHT WITH THE BOO VIBES

Love is beautiful and should smell beautiful. The mystery, the first date, the flirting, the adventure, and the fun—all of those moments can be accentuated by scented candles. There is something romantic, alluring, and sexy about a flame and being surrounded by a gorgeous scent. Whether it's date night with your long-standing lover, the first romantic date with someone you're interested in, or a relaxed singles mingle party, you can use the power of scent to elevate the moment.

I remember growing up with great romantic comedies from the 1990s and early 2000s. A lot of those movies had scenes with people cooking dinner for each other, cuddling on a couch, sharing a glass of wine, enjoying the nightlife in a beautiful city, or staying at a suite in a luxury hotel. I've always wondered how those moments smelled and, in my mind, I made up fragrances for all of those scenes.

SCENT NOTES

Dates are the perfect occasion to pull out deep notes like leather, oud, ash, and smoke, but it's nice to lighten them up a little by adding some sweetness like vanilla (the good kind) or rose, and a little spiciness like incense or pink pepper. The goal is to create a fun, enchanting, flirtatious, and comfortable environment. This is the perfect time to employ your scent-layering skills (see page 107). You could also pick out the scents with your date and decide what you want to light—some collaborative flirting, if you will. Here are some notes I enjoy:

- OUD: This rich, resiny, deep, woody, and sweet smell is a staple in luxury fragrances all around the world and makes for the perfect date-night fragrance. This note elevates your home into a magical space.

- INCENSE: Spicy, herbal, and sometimes resiny, incense is elevating as well as meditative. Known for its healing properties, the smell of burning incense creates a space that feels welcoming for deep and connecting conversations.

- ROSE: This is one of my favorite notes of all time. Rose can feel dated, but in the right combinations, rose is delicate, sweet, uplifting, and luxurious. A great rose note scent feels like the middle of spring, when flowers are in full bloom, and you wonder how life could get any sweeter.

PLACEMENT

You want to place this candle right on the dinner table or somewhere close enough that the candle scent interacts with your conversation in an intimate way.

OUTDOOR HANGOUT VIBES

Some people like to save their candles for the evenings, but I believe there is always a time and place for candles, even during the day. Scentscaping your day-to-day experiences can elevate those moments even more, especially when they're outdoor daytime brunches, outdoor chilling on the patio, baby showers, backyard brunches, or hanging by the pool (yes, you can get strongly scented outdoor candles).

SCENT NOTES

Balsamy and powdery scents are great for outdoor occasions. They mix in with the air outside to create a magical scentscape. Rose and musk are not always people's favorites because of their powdery and milky-skin scent notes, but I think they're less intense outdoors and really add a dimension of color and softness to any event. Here are some notes I would use.

- BALSAM FIR: This scent is not just for the holidays; the fresh-cut wood with juicy earthiness will make any situation feel welcoming and festive.

- ROSE: This widely used note gets a bad rap for not smelling young, but delicate rose scents can be gorgeous, flirty, freeing, and very uplifting. The world always smells prettier with rose.

- MUSK: The magic of powdery skin–scented nothingness is a staple for fragrances and, as part of an event's decor, musk in a candle adds a subtle elegance.

PLACEMENT

You can have so much fun using candles at daytime outdoor events. Of course, you can place them on any dining tables, but I would urge you to place them on a more elevated surface to keep the flame away from your guests. You can put the candles in corners of the patio or at the entrances to outside areas to create a stunning sensory entrance and exit. Really big candles from brands like Voluspa and diptyque, with multiple wicks, would do well here. Just be careful not to leave your candle burning if there is a draft or wind, because your candle might go out or start burning unevenly (more on uneven burning on page 63).

SPRING CLEANING VIBES

There's something about fresh, crisp scents that motivates me to get my life together. Every now and then, I wake up on a Saturday morning excited about doing a deeper clean than normal, but when I don't feel motivated to clean my apartment, I turn to the magic of scent to get the vibes right and energize myself to get it done. Before doing my laundry, scrubbing, sweeping, and wiping surfaces down, I like to light a candle that has a zesty and uplifting scent. Pair your refreshing candle with an upbeat playlist and you'll find yourself having cleaned the whole house in no time.

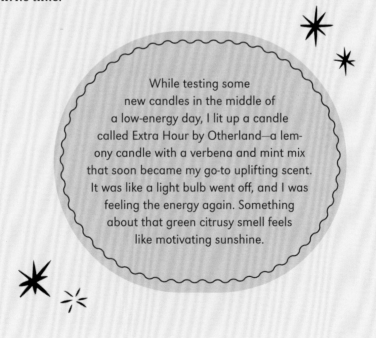

While testing some new candles in the middle of a low-energy day, I lit up a candle called Extra Hour by Otherland—a lemony candle with a verbena and mint mix that soon became my go-to uplifting scent. It was like a light bulb went off, and I was feeling the energy again. Something about that green citrusy smell feels like motivating sunshine.

SCENT NOTES

This is a time for your space to feel and smell fresh. Look for scents like fresh citrus, something green like mint or eucalyptus, or something pleasantly sharp, like ginger. This is not the time for cozy and relaxing scents like amber or sandalwood, because the next thing you know, you're lying on the couch getting cozy instead of doing all the work you need to do.

- LEMON: This is the refresher of all refreshers. Just like the fruit, lemon scents add a fresh, zesty sparkle to any situation.

- NEROLI: This floral, citrusy, and a little bit bitter scent smells like a great scrub-down.

- PETITGRAIN: Think citrus, but green and sharp. This scent comes from the bitter orange tree leaf and feels like playing outside in the early morning on a spring day.

- MINT: Aromatic, green, and, of course, minty. I rarely find candles with mint, but when I do, I must try them—it's the perfect soothing note.

- GINGER: Any candles with ginger smell like a refreshing Moscow mule cocktail on a hot day. It's such a fun, uplifting scent.

PLACEMENT

When cleaning, I like to place my candles as close to the action as possible: the kitchen, bathroom, or living room. While you shouldn't place candles next to the AC, a fan, or near an open window, because strong airflow may cause the candle to burn unevenly, I do like to have a little fresh air flowing to help the scent circulate more and ensure that I get whiffs as I move around.

END-OF-YEAR HOLIDAY VIBES

The end of the year should smell magical. After having made it through another year of life, I believe in channeling celebration. You made it. For holiday scents, you can go the traditional route with notes of fir, pine, and cinnamon, which are found in most holiday-scented candles. Those candles smell like nostalgia, as well as a hopeful future filled with love and friends. But I personally like to take those notes and add in deep, daring notes like bourbon and cognac and even juicy notes like cherry and stone fruit. The combination is a little untraditional, but why not have some fun?

SCENT NOTES

You can't really go wrong with sticking to the classic holiday scents, but for some reason, I find that these candles tend to be super smelly. Maybe it's the paraffin wax that helps throw the scent, or that the cooler months in the Northern Hemisphere are peak candle-buying season, so brands want to make sure customers get their money's worth. Either way, this high demand for holiday scents can sometimes lead to a strong scent but non-clean burn, so make sure that you buy a candle that burns cleanly in order to get the full scent experience (refer to page 36 on wax blends and candle scents). Here are some notes I love for the holidays:

- PINE: It's aromatic, out-doorsy, and crisp. The essential oil from pine needles makes for the perfect spicy wood note that is a quintessential element of the holidays.

- CINNAMON: The perfect cozy spice. Just like in pies, lattes, and desserts, cinnamon in a candle will make your home smell like an artisanal bakery that everyone wants to go to.

- BOURBON: This is the classic smell of deep luxury and unbothered relaxation. The sweet, deep, liquor aroma, when combined with vanilla, makes for the perfect inviting scent.

- CHERRY: This sweet, berry-forward scent is like the one sugary cocktail you drink to get the party started.

- BALSAM FIR: A camphora-ceous but sweet smell with a woody trail. Feels like being in the woods sur-rounded by evergreen trees with a splash of soothing sweetness.

PLACEMENT

Years ago, I was at a corporate holiday party that was fun but didn't smell amazing. With so many people packed into the space, it smelled more like a bar than a warm and inviting affair. To avoid this issue for your own gathering, try placing holiday candles in the places where your guests will be congregating. The best parties have places to dance, mingle, and relax, so I believe in "fragrancing" those areas accordingly. For the main mingling areas, tried-and-true balsam fir candles are perfect—this is what people expect. For the dancing space and the midnight-kiss-under-the-mistletoe areas, I would add in something a bit juicier or woodier like stone fruit, oud, or cedarwood.

CHILLIN' WITH THE HOMIES VIBES

Don't you just love a good dinner party with friends? I once went to a friend's house party in Los Angeles. He has a gorgeous home, and he had mentioned how much he loves candles. I didn't realize just how much he loved them until I entered the party. There were candles burning everywhere. Multiple candles in multiple rooms. I was in heaven enjoying all the scents, telling people what made each scent so wonderful. As the night wore on, I saw people settle into different rooms for conversations, games, and cocktail-making. I remember thinking how amazing it was that scent was an unseen but important character of this party for every guest and every interaction.

That party is where I learned the art of "scentscaping a party." A night of cooking, delicious craft cocktails, and great conversations is pure joy to me. To take that joy up a notch, I like to light different candles around my home to complement my gatherings. Something here for the friends having a deep conversation in the nook, something there for the friends finalizing the meal in the kitchen, something elsewhere for the group playing board games in the living room, and don't forget something to keep the bathroom smelling fresh.

SCENT NOTES

There are different types of parties and spaces to consider when scentscaping a gathering. Here are some general scent notes I love, but feel free to switch things up or cater your scents to the theme of your gathering, like using leather, whiskey, and smoky candles for a Roaring Twenties party, or patchouli for a sixties-themed party.

- TOBACCO is a great note. I don't smoke, but the smell of tobacco mixed with vanilla or cognac in a candle reminds me of luxury hotel lobbies of yore. There is something grown-up, sexy, and exciting about that smell.

- RUM, BOURBON, or WHISKEY— similar to tobacco, there is a maturity to the smell of these liquor-inspired scents. They're assuring, fun, and relaxed.

- LEATHER is one of my favorite scents because it smells like an old library. The books, the leather chairs, the wood—they all point toward understated luxury.

- SMOKE and ASH are in my top ten notes of all time. The deep fireplace and old-burnt-log scent profile reminds me of the morning after an amazing night. Last night's conversations and jokes. The almost sweet and smoky memory of the best times of life.

- CANNABIS, with its green, ashy, soothing note, is so alluring, grounding, and relaxing, even for this non-smoker. It's perfect for that deep late-night conversation with a friend about the meaning of life and the wonders of the world.

- PALO SANTO, VETIVER, and CLARY SAGE are just the right relaxing notes to end the night on.

PLACEMENT

Candle placement at parties is really fun! Your home is like a canvas, and the candles are the paint, so you can create whatever space you want for the backdrop for your party. In the living room, I believe in scent-layering, so I would put candles on the coffee table, side tables, and on top of cabinets. The more the merrier, but make sure that the scents complement one another. I would recommend testing out the layering before your friends arrive. In the kitchen, the center island is great for a candle, or somewhere close to the stove top to diffuse cooking smells. For the bathroom, I put candles on top of the toilet tank, and I like to pair that candle with a strong diffuser. Lastly, you can place candles outside as well; just make sure that they have a heavy scent in case of any breezes. And always monitor your outdoor candles!

THE ART AND JOY OF SCENT LAYERING

Embrace your inner
scent artist! Candles typically
have a number of notes that come
together to create a unique scent, but you can
create your own by lighting multiple candles at the
same time to make something interesting that is just for
you. Here's how to layer your own scents:

1 | Start with a signature base-scented candle.

2 | Light it and let its scent fill up the room.

3 | In the same room as the lit signature candle, sniff some of your
other candles to get a sense of whether the combination works.

4 | When you find one you like, light it and let the scents merge!

When you're starting out, try working with some classic combinations like sandalwood and rose or vanilla and leather or fig and
a wood. As you become more comfortable layering scents, try
thinking outside the box to create a combination that is right
for your home. I personally love a combination of fig and
stone fruit, an opopanax (sweet resin smell) with an ash
note, or a clean linen paired with something with fruit
notes. Weird and wonderful is the way! Sometimes
it goes wrong—that's life—but remember
that you can always try again. All is
fair in love and scents.

UNCOMMON SCENTS I LOVE

There are a few notes
I love that are not readily available in retail outlets, but if you come
across them, you should give them a shot:

• **OPOPANAX**: This is a resin that is sweet, smoky,
and a little powdery. It's my secret weapon
when I want to impress fragrance heads.

• **AMBROXAN**: This is a synthetic compound for amber
that's muskier and drier. It's the main note in a candle by
Juliette Has a Gun called "Not a Candle." It's so specific
and interesting. Some people call it a fragrance enhancer
or a modern-day amber, but either way, I love it.

• **ASH**: A lot of people like a woody or smoky scent,
but I particularly love a deep ashy, scrape-
the-bottom-of-the-fireplace scent. It's
deep, grounding, and burns
surprisingly clean.

CANDLES FOR WELLNESS AND SELF-CARE

The world can feel so off-center sometimes. With demands from work and family, the craziness on the news, and everything else, our minds are always running. One day, while in a virtual therapy session, I was becoming overwhelmed by trying to give voice to all my anxieties. My therapist instructed me to stop for a minute, light one of my candles, lie down on the couch, and take a few deep breaths, in and out, while focusing on the scent and what I was feeling. After about ten minutes, I could feel my shoulders relax, my breath was deeper and slower, and my mind was a little clearer. I got back up and we continued the session. Yes, I still had the same problems, but because my mind was less frazzled, I was able to articulate what I was feeling more clearly. What he had just done was make me aware of situations where I'm in a heightened moment of stress and show me how to take action to anchor myself with something that I enjoy.

I'm not a professional wellness expert, but in my case, I find it incredibly effective to use candles and their scent to ground and re-center myself. There's something about the combination of a gentle glow and beautiful scent that makes for the perfect moment to exhale. And don't we all need a moment to stop and re-center ourselves every now and then? Scent has a powerful impact on how we feel, and if we scent our space in the right way, we can help ourselves relax and wind down our minds.

We so often turn to our other senses to ease our discomfort, such as eating comfort foods and listening to some calming music. Or we exercise. All of these are valid ways to decompress, but if you haven't tried aroma-therapy, I urge you to consider investing in scent as another way to ease stress.

Here are a few ways I love to use candles in rituals of self-care.

MEDITATION

I NEED A MOMENT

I used to find meditation very hard. I downloaded all the apps, went to so many sessions, and tried different methods, but I was never able to slow my mind down enough to benefit from it. At the end of my meditation session, I would find myself more stressed.

This changed one day, in an unexpected way, when I looked at myself in the mirror and I didn't recognize or like what I saw. I wasn't looking or feeling like the vibrant person I used to be. I had overworked myself, I had stopped doing things I was passionate about, and I had let myself go a little. In the past, I would have signed up for a personal trainer, tried to change my diet, and forced myself to get myself together, but this time I just didn't have the energy. I felt like my life was stalling. I turned to a book I had read many times before called *You Can Heal Your Life*, by Louise Hay. This book is all about loving yourself back to health. Deep self-love.

Somewhere in the book, the author talks about creating rituals filled with self-love and performing them daily. One of those things was engaging with positive affirmations, and I started doing the affirmations while burning candles. Affirmations can feel weird at first, especially when you're saying them to yourself in the mirror, but what did I have to lose? I would push myself to do these affirmations every day and then spend the next five minutes sitting still with the candles burning, focusing on breathing and the scent. Lo and behold, I started being able to meditate and stay focused—the fragrance was my way forward. The next time you're meditating, try lighting a candle and you may experience a different level of calm.

SCENTS

I like my meditation fragrances to be calming but uplifting. This is not the time to burn a candle that's too strong, because it may be distracting. Soothing notes like sage or palo santo or fresh and cleansing notes like neroli or tangerine are personal favorites. I may layer the candles or burn them alongside some actual incense too. Here are some notes I like for meditation.

- PALO SANTO: A soothing, subtly sweet woody note that smells like a luxury desert retreat.

- SAGE: An earthy, fresh, peppery, and green scent that feels like a deep breath in the middle of a grassy plain.

- TANGERINE: Zesty, citrusy, and sweet with a little tartness that's like a physical pick-me-up.

- FRANKINCENSE: Woody, piney, earthy, and complex with a little sweet resin that is super centering.

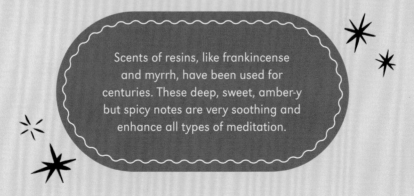

Scents of resins, like frankincense and myrrh, have been used for centuries. These deep, sweet, amber-y but spicy notes are very soothing and enhance all types of meditation.

INVITING GRATITUDE

LETTING IT ALL OUT

I, like a lot of people, benefit from writing down my thoughts to help figure out my feelings. I've been journaling since my teens, and now I keep a gratitude journal that I write in every night. I grew up watching *The Oprah Winfrey Show*, and one of the ways she cultivated living an abundant life was by being grateful. If Oprah taught it, I did it. And wow, it's true. Every night, I write down five things that happened that day that I am grateful for. It could be a small thing, like when a stranger smiled at me on the street or when I felt the sun on my face on my way to get my morning coffee, or it could be a really big thing, such as a work presentation that went well, or it could be something deep, like feeling healthy and strong. Without fail, I go to sleep feeling centered and uplifted. Gratitude is an expense-free way to find some joy in the day and help ease some of the tension you may be feeling before you continue on to the next day.

I know it may sound a little idealistic to be this intentional about hopes, dreams, gratitude, and candle scents, but I've found that acknowledging my gratitude has enriched my life, and I wish for you to find the same enrichment.

SCENTS

The scents that enhance your gratitude practice should be both sturdy and expressive. You want them to help you feel grounded in the moment, but also emotionally open. Choosing them is almost like being in an art class. You need the easel and canvas to set the stage (woody and green notes) and then the colors to bring your ideas to life (florals and other sweet notes). These are a few notes I believe are great to burn when journaling:

- TEAKWOOD: Woody, bold, warm, and masculine, teakwood is a pleasant, earthy aroma that invites calm and focus.

- LAVENDER: Powdery, sweet, herbal, green, and some-times camphor-forward, lavender is one of my favorites because it almost instantly relaxes me and creates a great mood for getting my thoughts down.

- MOSS: Earthy, wet, and a little amber-y, this note is like taking a hike in a green forest on a rainy day. Just as you would clear your thoughts on a hike, moss notes help you do that while journaling.

- FIG: I'm obsessed with fig notes in everything: candles, room sprays, fine fragrance. Green, creamy, and slightly sweet, fig smells like luxury.

- MINT: Cool, herbal, fresh, and green, mint gives you the boost you need. Smell-ing a mint candle is like getting off the phone with a friend who has just given you the best pep talk.

- WHITE FLORALS: I love the soft, feminine, rich, and sometimes powdery scents of tuberose, gardenia, lily, or anything in that realm. It's like being in a garden, mesmerized by the beauty of the world.

UNWINDING

LET'S CALL IT A WRAP

So many of us don't have good sleep habits. Too many of us are staring at screens close to bedtime—TVs, phones, tablets— which keeps our brains too engaged to settle properly. On top of that, I often find my mind racing with thoughts from the past day and worries about the next day. One of the solutions, according to sleep experts, is to create a sleep routine to allow yourself time to unwind at least an hour before you go to bed. Because of this, I've cultivated a very specific wind-down process for myself at the end of the night. An hour before I go to bed, I light a candle in my room, turn down the AC to a very cool temperature, and let the cold air and scent mix to create the perfect atmosphere for my nighttime routine.

I know we are all addicted to our phones, afraid of missing out on happenings on social media, the latest news, the next funny video, and just generally wanting to feel connected to other people. But the best connection is the one we have with ourselves. Try to set aside some time every night to connect with yourself without any external distractions. Just peace and quiet (or a gentle playlist with some R&B vibes or soft pop), a relaxing candle, and a grounding practice. There is nothing quite as magical as reading a book (yes, a real book) on a midweek evening. Or maybe you're someone who enjoys the ritual of an end-of-night skin-care routine. Either way, the key is to take a moment for yourself while also doing something great for your body.

Light a candle and take the time to give yourself the rest you need and deserve. Your body will thank you.

SCENTS

The best unwinding scents are soothing, soft, and sensual and leave you feeling lighter instead of overwhelmed with fragrance. I like to pick a candle that is lightly scented but still luxurious, like cashmere, soft musk, a light rose, or even amber. These fragrances smell the way a soft and fluffy sweatshirt feels, and that's what I'm looking for in those unwinding moments. I don't like the fragrances to be too strong, because they may engage my senses too much and make me feel more awake rather than sleepy. The goal is to create a scented relaxation bubble. Here are some notes I like when I'm getting ready for bed:

- CASHMERE: Soft, slightly musky, sandalwood, and a little bit of vanilla. This smells like luxury in a sensual and soft way.

- MUSK: Powdery, powerful but still delicate, dry, and a little earthy. Sometimes called a "skin scent," a little bit of musk in a candle makes for an intimate and sweet moment.

- ROSE: There are many types of rose scents, but for unwinding, you want a rose that is powdery, light, and slightly sweet. You want an airy, floaty rose, not the whole rose garden.

- VANILLA: For nighttime, stay away from the bakery smells and instead get a candle with a solid vanilla base and other soothing but non-sweet notes in the middle and top.

- CEDARWOOD: This is my ultimate soothing scent. It's camphoraceous, woody, soft, and cooling. I find it irresistible and calming, like putting a chest rub on and feeling relief in your airways.

• GRASSY: There is nothing more relaxing to me than being in a large open space with a green, woody, earthy, and sunny feeling. Like looking at endless blue skies and feeling the majesty of the vastness of the world, inhaling this note is uplifting without being too invigorating.

MANIFESTATION

MAKING YOUR DREAMS COME TRUE

One Sunday out of the month, I like to take a break from social gatherings, working, and other tasks and focus on my life vision, goals, and progress so far. Many who know me would call me an intense person, because I like to be clear about my goals, but I prefer to call myself a focused and intentional person. In any case, being clear about what I want and how I want my life to look has treated me well. (Funnily enough, a few years ago, I wrote that I wanted to write a book and here we are, so I guess it works.) I used to do all my goal-tracking on a spreadsheet, meticulously plotting progress updates and next steps, but this became too daunting and took the joy away from the process of achieving the goal. Now, I try to write down how I feel about my progress and where I am going in a physical journal. There is something about putting a pen to paper rather than typing on a keyboard that allows my thoughts, feelings, and intentions to connect. When I do this, I like to light either a grounding candle, with maybe a deep teakwood note that reminds me of a beautiful old study, or something green and floral that reminds me of a park where I imagine myself sitting on the grass under a shady tree writing down my dreams. I much prefer this new journaling approach and recommend it; you can use candles to create the scenes you need to let your thoughts flow onto the page. Scentscape your life with candles to create the canvas on which to paint your dream life.

SCENTS

I like to create a magical and mystical feeling when I'm thinking about my dreams and setting new goals. Here are some ethereal but grounding notes that evoke an enchanting optimism when I'm manifesting good things for the future:

- OUD: Known as "liquid gold," oud is deeply sweet, sometimes smoky, and intense. A lot of people think of seduction and sensuality when they think of oud, but I think the richness and mysterious elements of the note also make for great late-night vision boarding.

- IRIS: Often described as a powdery, damp, and smooth floral note, this smell is also very romantic in an introspective and reflective way. This note feels like true and gentle optimism.

- SAFFRON: One of the oldest, most complex, and most expensive perfume ingredients, saffron is slightly sweet, leathery, and a little bitter but also earthy. With its naturally luxurious qualities, it makes sense that saffron is perfect for manifesting abundance.

- INCENSE: Incense can be made from different forms of gums and resins, not just frankincense. I love the rich, intense, spicy smell of incense. It reminds me of a vacation where you go with the intention to "find yourself" and end up roaming the streets, unexpectedly making new friends, and trying new flavors. It's wanderlust in a smell.

- TEAKWOOD: A rich, spicy, comforting, and warm wood that brings an earthy presence to your space. This note feels both natural and refined at the same time. Fun fact: The oil from teakwood is also used for medicinal purposes—all the better for manifesting health and wealth.

STYLING
YOUR
CANDLES

Let's take it up a notch! The joy of candles goes beyond the scent and extends to your home decor. Yes, candles smell wonderful, but I believe that they should also look amazing. Having beautiful candles in your home can elevate your space and your scent experience. This is one of my favorite parts of loving and living with candles. The infinite array of beautiful vessels allows for so many decor options that will bring your home's style together.

There are so many styling options to consider. You can choose between vessel types (glass or ceramic, or tin for fans of farmhouse chic), label designs (regular labels, foil, printed), and even use some accessories (cloches, wick trimmers, and trays). Channel your inner interior designer and have some fun!

CHIC

A CLASSIC AESTHETIC

When I was looking for my first solo apartment, I was in my mid-twenties and I gravitated toward ultramodern spaces with sleek white walls and sharp corners. I've since moved on to liking more cozy, comfortable, and contemporary spaces, but in that first apartment, everything had to be modern and crisp. Even the candles I liked back then were like that: They had simple and clean labels, mostly black and white vessels, and the scents usually had one or two main notes. Even though time has opened me up to different styles, this classic aesthetic is calming, feels grown up, and never goes out of style.

HOW TO STYLE

Style these modern spaces with large simple candles with bold black and white labels. Stick to simple vessel types with clear or frosted glass, or try concrete, porcelain, or ceramic vessels with minimal designs if you want to play with textures and materials. In addition to traditional, you can get intricately molded vessels or square vessels to add some interest.

PLACEMENT

I like to put modern candles next to a vase of fresh, white flowers for a classic look. They also look elegant placed on your coffee table atop some striking and design-forward books that showcase your interests and create points of conversation in your home.

To be dressy, I love adding candles to gorgeous clear hurricanes or cloches. This approach feels like you've created your own department-store display in your home. A row of cloches featuring your favorite candles is so beautiful, striking, and timeless. This area will be a place where people gather and discuss the scents, making your home a great place to connect with guests.

LUXURY

IT'S GIVING OPULENCE

Growing up, my parents always said I had expensive taste. It's funny to me, because I didn't have the money for the expensive taste I had, but I was always attracted to luxury. So, I guess becoming Sir Candle Man and loving luxury candles makes sense. They were right. It's not that I was attracted to the price that you had to pay for something, but I loved the feeling of treating myself and being in spaces that felt luxurious because, even as a young man, I believed in taking care of myself. You know that feeling when you enter a fancy hotel lobby, a boutique store, or a friend's gorgeous home? That opulent feeling is one I live for, because the beauty is overwhelming in the best possible way.

HOW TO STYLE

There are two ways to achieve an opulent look with candles. One is to buy simple and less expensive candles and then style around them. Another is to buy intricate luxury candles and use them as the starting point for your decor. I like option two, because I prefer to focus on the candle first, but both work as long as the candles look fly!

You should look for candles that both smell and look luxurious. Gold is your friend here: gold vessels, gold labels, gold accents. Some say gold is gaudy, but I think gold is classic if it's not overdone. Depending on the type of luxury you like, I think adding some greenery from plants around the candles makes for a sexy, moody, jungle-type room. Green and gold looks lush and expensive.

PLACEMENT

If you're going for luxury, why not let it be seen? I like my luxury-candle decor moments to be focal points in the living room, dining room, or entrance area. You can add the candles to the center of your spaces, but I think having moments of luxury sprinkled across your rooms is better. I like to group candles together to create a stacked and full space. Try putting them on a gold tray next to some intricate lamps or other decorative items like gold wick trimmers, wick dippers, and lighters. Don't be shy here—for this look, more is more.

QUIRKY

COLOR, COLOR, COLOR

Something happened to me in 2020, during the early days of the COVID-19 pandemic. I had typically lived a fast life, so I hadn't spent much time decorating my apartment. I was never there. With the move to working from home and having to spend a lot of time at home, I realized that I didn't love my space because it was so dry and boring. I decided to move to a new apartment. I found a place that was less square and modern but more cute and charming. The charming apartment had old hardwood floors, crown molding, and intricate tiling, and it felt like the great restart I needed. As part of this new era, I wanted to add more color to my life. Aside from artwork, plants, and furniture, I made sure to have some colored candle vessels as well. I feel like a whole other person compared to the old me in the dreary apartment. My life has been so much better since I started living in color, and I suggest you try it if you're looking for something to uplift you. You have the power to bring color and vibrance into your life.

HOW TO STYLE

There are lots of ways to add color and joy via candles: colored vessels, colored waxes, and colored accessories. Some of my favorite candles come in very colorful and intricately designed vessels. Ornate prints, colored glass, stained concrete, colorful porcelain—the list is endless. You should allow yourself to play! For a bold decor moment, a black wax is striking and iconic. People will notice the drama of the black wax. For more festive spaces, yellow, blue, and green are great additions. Choose whatever strikes your fancy to bring your home to life.

PLACEMENT

I like to have color-centered rooms and moments. For a room that has a dedicated color scheme—for example, a blue room—simply adding in a blue candle (vessel or wax) is very chic, cool, and seamless. Other times, for example, for a dinner party, I will have different colored candles in different spaces to bring the mood of the home to life. Color is to be enjoyed, so place it anywhere you want a pop of joy in the room.

HOW TO REMOVE WAX FROM VESSELS

I love reusing candle vessels, especially colorful ones. This is a great way to be sustainable while adding practical decor to your home. All you have to do is remove the wax, clean the vessel, remove the label (if you want to), then use it for anything you want.

There are lots of ways to remove wax from a vessel. For glass vessels, you can melt the wax with a candle lamp warmer or blow-dryer, throw out the melted wax, let the glass container cool down, and then clean out any remaining wax with soap and water. Another almost foolproof method is to place the vessel in the freezer overnight—this will shrink the wax a little bit. The next day, turn the vessel upside down and the wax should pop right out. Finish by washing your vessel with soap and water.

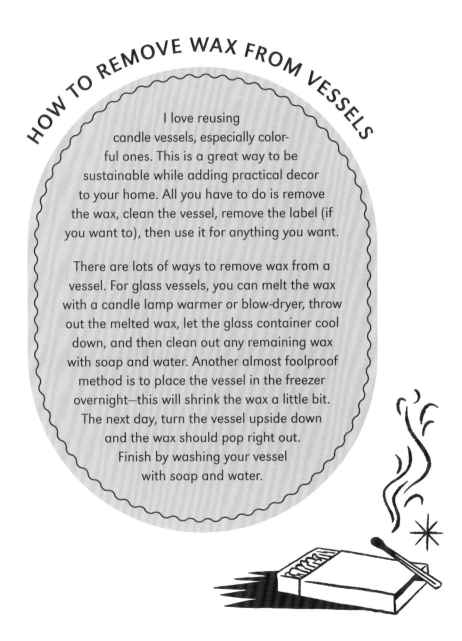

CHILL

IT'S JUST VIBES

I love going on vacation, and I specifically like an island or resort vacation that feels relaxed and free with a bohemian look. You know, the woven mats, baskets, plants, ceramics. That always on-trend boho-chic aesthetic. To me, this feels like the ultimate escape and like a deep exhale after a stressful week. Sometimes just seeing spaces that look like the types of vacations I love is enough to help me relax.

HOW TO STYLE

The key to a bohemian candle look is to keep everything loose. You can have lots of items like candles, plants, woven baskets, cement vessels, rugs, and more, but you can't have them too close together. The space between them allows for movement and freedom.

PLACEMENT

You can do this on a mantel, on a sparsely decorated shelf, or in a really big room. You should be careful not to light a candle too close to woven baskets or rugs, because they can catch fire pretty quickly. We don't want to burn the place down!

BOLD

YOU'RE A STAR!

When I was in my early teens, I was shy and reserved. I didn't like people looking at me or talking about me. I hated standing out or experiencing anything that would make me feel singled out. This was most likely because I always felt different. As an adult, I'm still reserved but not as shy. It took me twenty-five years on this earth to come out, another five years to fully love myself, and another five years (so now, haha) to stand boldly in who I am and show myself to the world.

Life is so much better when you show up as your full self. One of the ways I show up as *my* full self is by talking about my deep love for fragrance and candles. Although having a candle passion can be pretty niche, I love being me, and I love choosing bold, standout, investment-piece candles to display in my home.

HOW TO STYLE

Want to go bold? Get yourself some massive candles. Some brands have candles that are hundreds of ounces and burn for extended hours—the ultimate statement piece! These candles are typically best-seller fragrances and come in special-edition or newly designed vessels, and they generally have multiple wicks because of the size of the candle and wax surface area. If you've never tried one, you should. This is a way to invest in yourself and show the world how much you love yourself . . . and how much you love candles.

PLACEMENT

Indoors, I like to place these big candles on top of a chest or as a single item on side tables. Just make sure the table is sturdy, because these candles are heavy. If you have lots of corners or nooks in your home, you can place them in a corner instead of filling that space with a planter. Once you are done burning these big vessels (it will take a while), you can use the containers as bougie trash cans, planters, or, as someone once said, as a champagne bucket—genius!

ACKNOWLEDGMENTS

This book is a dream come true, and I'm so grateful. In 2019, I wrote on my vision board that I wanted to write a book, and I can't believe we did it! Thank you to Chronicle Books for bringing love and light to this idea, and thank you to my editor, Cristina Garces, for believing in me from the beginning and making this journey so fulfilling. You've helped me be more confident in my dreams. You told me I could do it and I did. To the design team, I'm so thankful. Cristina told me the book would look beautiful because that's what Chronicle does, and she was right.

Thank you to my incredible Sir Candle Man community. You make living with and loving candles so fun and creative. This journey has been one of the most unexpected and joyful experiences of my life.

Thank you to my team. Thank you to my agents, Alexandra Emmerman and Sophie Kavanagh. Thank you to Chris Sawtelle and Brian Nelson, the first people in the industry to believe in me and push me to make my dreams a reality. You saw me before anyone else. Thank you to Helen Yu, my powerhouse lawyer and friend. Thank you to Rees and Gina for making Sir Candle Man global.

Thank you to my friends and family, who just went with me on my Sir Candle Man journey and didn't judge me when I said I would be diving deep into candles. My sister, Chido, for hearing me talk about candles every other day. My brother, Farai, and my sister-in-law, Chebet, thank you. To my parents, thank you for letting me be me. Thank you, Tiffany, Kevin, Michael Modon, Alexandra Khoury Modon, Nina, Nieman, Chika, Dre, Kara, Brian Feit, Krista, EJ, Michael Martino, Rez, Alex Rocca, Sarah Aleem, Dawn Kamerling, Dan Liss, Matt Carmona, Kyle Hanagami, Keith (my amazing trainer who checks up on Sir Candle Man), and

Ethan Karetsky. Thank you to Saron and Julia, who pushed me into the candle business. Thank you to Tarek Ali for reminding me that "yes, I am a writer" when I was doubting myself.

To my work colleagues and friends, Isabel, Steff, CeCe, Joyce, Shadi, Leah, Ally, and Sophie, thank you. Thank you, Bryan Thoensen, for pushing me to explore my full creativity as a professional. Thank you, Dan Habashi and Vanessa Craft, for always supporting Sir Candle Man.

Thank you to my teachers, the candle-brand owners, Abigail Cook-Stone, Jon Bresler, Mary Ann Murphy, Sarah Hart, Teri Johnson, Matthew Herman, Brice the Candle Guy and Candle Delirium, Kristen and Tom, Dara Weiss, Priscilla Camacho, Holly Davies, Laura Slatkin, Courteney Cox, Sarah Jahnke, Corentin and Arash, Phil Riportella, Bryan Edwards, Taylor Swaim, Jess Raffo, Melissa Smith, Brianna Lipovsky, Gavin Luxe, Reis Chester, Erica Werber, August and Piers Founders, Paige Casey, Alyssa Tomasetti, Alyx Tunno, Steven Cutajar, Erwan Raguenes, Chrissy Fichtl, Jackie Aina, and Denis Asamoah. Thank you to my internet fragrance friends for keeping me inspired: Jade, Rekeema, Funmi Monet, Emma Vernon; Isaac Lekach, David Pirrotta, Chelito Albanese Villaflor, Nils Beeman, Tembe Denton-Hurst, Claire Pelitier, and Medgina Saint-Elien for giving me a mainstream voice, and Varshini Satish.

Thank you to Angella Choe for capturing my essence.

Thank you to Linda Levy and the Fragrance Foundation for uncovering the world of fragrance for me. I will forever be grateful.

I love you all!

Illuminate your life,

Sir Candle Man

LIT

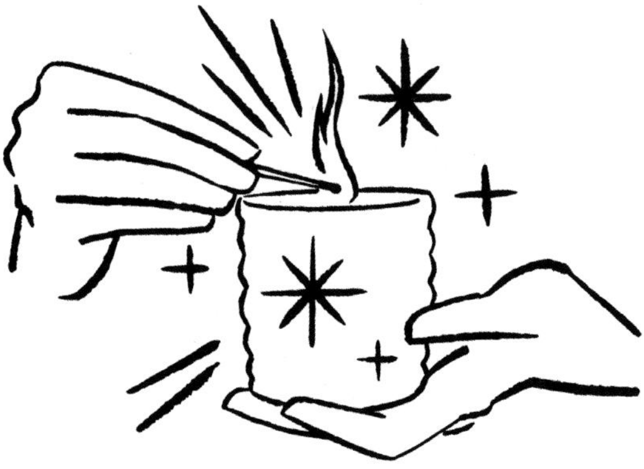